Remembering Gran

Copyright © 2002 John Hunt Publishing Ltd.

Text © 2002 Jacqueline Harding

Illustrations © 2002 Margaret Brampton

ISBN 1 84298 087 4

Designed by
ANDREW MILNE DESIGN

Write to John Hunt Publishing Ltd
46a West Street, Alresford, Hampshire SO24 9AU, UK

The rights of Jacqueline Harding as author and Margaret Brampton as illustrator
of this work have been asserted in accordance with the Copyright,
Designs and Patents Act 1988.

A CIP catalogue record for this book is available from the British Library.

CARE for Education produces educational resources for nursery, primary and
secondary schools, gives guidance and training for teachers and school
governors/board members; facilitates conferences and seminars, and works on
educational policy with Government, local authorities, schools and parents.
Practice and policy work focuses on areas such as early years, school exclusion,
sex and relationships education and school management.

These Early Years books are part of the **Celebrating Marriage** resources
launched in 2001/2. More details of these resources can be found on the
website: www.celebratingmarriage.com

Printed in China

Remembering Gran

Jacqueline Harding

Illustrated by
Margaret Brampton

John Hunt
Publishing Limited

'I remember that holiday!' I said.

'It was such fun.'

Gran laughed, 'And, I remember how wet we all got when Ted fell into the river.'

'Woof!' said Ted, as if he remembered it well.

Every photo seemed to be packed with memories of fun and laughter. I loved looking through the old photo album with Gran.

I visited Gran most days after school.

The smell of freshly baked cakes seemed to greet me as I ran through the door.

'And what have you been doing today?' asked Gran.

She always asked the same question and I always replied,

'Not much!'

Then, we'd set about eating cakes, sorting out cupboards or drawing, and sometimes Gran would plait my hair.

As the years went by, I noticed that Gran seemed to be getting slower and slower.

'Come on Gran,' I'd say, 'I'll pour the tea for you!'

'Yes, go on dear,' she would say with a chuckle.

'You are so much quicker than me now a days!'

At times I would notice that her hands were shaking more than ever and she didn't always remember to do the things she'd promised.

Mum handed me a flask of soup to take to Gran's as she knew that Gran often forgot to eat.

'Gran's not getting any younger!' She would say.

In fact, I began to realise that mum was always saying that, and I wondered why.

'School Sports Day today,' called mum one morning.

'Great! I'll go and get my sports bag.' I said, 'and shall we collect Gran on the way?'

'Gran can't come as she's feeling very tired,' said mum, 'but I'll take lots of photos with your camera.'

I was happy about going to sports day but sad that Gran couldn't come.

Sport's day was great and I really liked winning!

I came first in the high jump and I helped my team to win by running fast in the relay race.

I felt important. It was so exciting and I wondered if every day could be as good as this.

Mum took lots of photos of me looking very happy. She promised to get them developed as soon as possible so that I could show Gran.

The next day I could hear mum on the telephone. She was saying something about calling the ambulance and packing things for Gran.

She didn't have time to explain anything to me. All that day at school I kept wondering what was wrong, if it was serious and whether Gran would be OK.

When I came home from school mum looked so very worried.

'Come and sit down,' mum beckoned to me, trying to smile bravely.

'Ted will have to stay the night with us, as Gran is very old and very tired. The Doctors at the hospital are looking after her well, but...' Mum's voice trailed off.

That night I tossed and turned and then suddenly I sat bolt upright.

Questions were racing through my mind but the most important question seemed to be, 'Did Gran see the photos of my Sports Day?'

When I came home from school the next day mum met me at the door.

Tears streamed down her face as she gently told me that Gran had died.

'She died peacefully in her sleep,' mum said softly.

I pushed past her as she was speaking, ran upstairs, slammed the door and burst into tears.

I was furious that every day wasn't like Sport's Day, cross that Gran had left us, lonely and sad – so very, very sad.

I think I must have cried all night, at least it felt like that.

In the morning mum woke me and just cuddled me. She didn't say anything and that was just what I needed. Then I told her how I felt. She listened quietly and that was good.

Ted wagged his tail when I came downstairs and I stroked him.

'What will happen to Ted?' I asked mum (until then I hadn't thought about him).

'Gran told me that she wanted you to have him,' said mum.

'Mine! He'll be my dog!'

I was so pleased.

After the funeral I went to Gran's house to help mum sort out her things.

It was a bit strange at first, I kept expecting to see Gran at any moment and when I picked her things up – they just smelt like her.

'This is for you,' said mum as she handed me the photo album, 'I know Gran would like you to have it.'

It fell open at the page of Sport's Day photos.

'Gran did see the photos!' I exclaimed happily.

Then, with tears and smiles I started to turn the pages. Ted sat next to me and we remembered the good times we'd had together.

'I remember that holiday' I said. 'It was such fun!'

Mum laughed, 'I remember how wet we all got when Ted fell into the river!'

'Woof!' said Ted, as if he remembered it well.

This book is best read to children individually, although, if appropriate it can be read sensitively to a small group of children.

It must be remembered that young children are capable of grieving in the same way as adult. They may go through similar stages of grief – for example, denial, anger, guilt and depression. They must be given the respect to grieve in their own way.

Give the child/children opportunity to respond and talk about their situation if they want to. Don't insist on a discussion. Sometimes children don't wish to comment at the time of hearing the story but might want to talk about it later in the day. It is perfectly OK for a child to cry and must be allowed to grieve in this way without being told to be brave.

This story can be linked to the Family Tree story.